DEC - 2023

For Wihl Guu Smeaax, my brother. A friend,
uncle, and son like no other.
—H.G. / B.D.H.

For John "Guy" Keenan (1946–2021),
in loving memory.
—N.D.

The Raven Mother

By Hetxw'ms Gyetxw (Brett D. Huson)

Illustrated by Natasha Donovan

HIGHWATER
PRESS

ABOVE

Warm rays of hloxs, the sun, stretch out from behind the mountains. Droplets of water hang in the air, forming mist as far as the eye can see. The scent of coniferous[1] trees and shrubs mixes with the fresh smell of moss and river water. High atop a peeling birch tree, Nox Gaak, the raven mother, stands out against the misty white landscape.

April is the time of Lasa ya'a, the Spring Salmon's Returning Home Moon. When the sun's rays cut through the mist, they reveal a landscape on the cusp[2] of blossoming. As the fog disperses,[3] we see Nox Gaak perched by her nest with two new chicks. Her lifelong partner is nearby, along with a few other ravens.

1 **Coniferous** trees have woody trunks and stems, often with needles for leaves.

2 The **cusp** is a point in time when something will change.

3 To **disperse** means to scatter in all directions.

¹ A **species** is a group of similar individuals that can reproduce.
² A **food web** is made up of all the food chains in a single ecosystem.

Lasa ya'a is also an exciting time of renewal for Gitxsan children. They have been eagerly awaiting the arrival of the spring salmon, so they can indulge in fresh salmon chowder. Hagwiltsum is a simple yet delicious soup of salmon, potatoes, onion, rice, seaweed, and, more recently, a touch of curry powder.

As the spring salmon are returning, so too do many other species[1] return to the land. This change signals a replenishing of the food web[2] that Nox Gaak and her family are a part of. This also means they will have access to a greater variety of food.

The raven chicks are new to the world outside of their shells. They are aggressively hungry, and it takes a community to satisfy them. Ravens are some of the best scavengers[1] in the animal kingdom, but they are also great hunters when they work together. Like the Gitxsan people, the ravens look after one another and help each other raise their young. For this reason, ravens can flourish[2] in almost every ecosystem.[3]

1 **Scavengers** are organisms that eat dead or decaying matter.
2 To **flourish** means to grow well.
3 An **ecosystem** refers to all of the organisms that live within and interact with a specific environment.

1 Young birds are **fledged** when their feathers and muscles are ready for flight.
2 A **cache** is a place for hiding, storing, or preserving food and supplies.
3 To **fertilize** means to add nutrients to the soil.

New Feathers

Lasa 'yan'tsa, the Budding Trees and Blooming Flowers Moon, passes over. It is May, and the new chicks have fledged[1] and are now taking short flights away from the nest. These young ravens have been watching Nox Gaak as she feeds, learning how to scavenge, hunt, and store food.

Ravens, along with their cousins, crows and jays, are hoarders. They store caches[2] of food all over their territory, and many become forgotten treasures. Buried seeds grow to be new trees and plants, and other hidden foods fertilize[3] the environment.

The ravens' ability to spread new growth across the land is what has led the Gitxsan to revere[1] them through song and story. As a creator and bringer of life, Nox Gaak has a storied[2] past to live up to and shares her knowledge with her growing young.

Although the fledglings[3] are now flying independently, they still depend on their parents to feed them and teach them. But their mother and father don't do this alone; other ravens in the group also watch the young ones and share food when they find it.

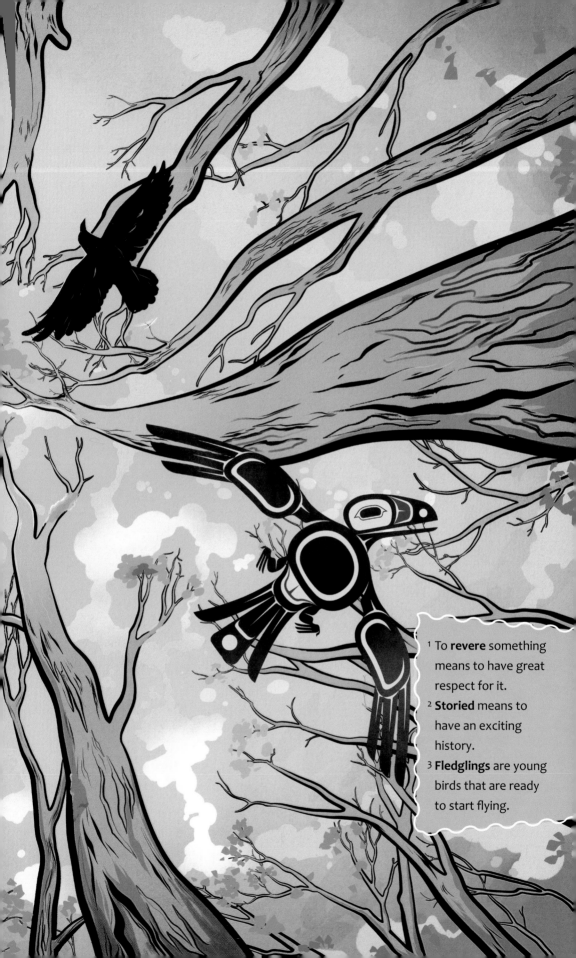

¹ To **revere** something means to have great respect for it.

² **Storied** means to have an exciting history.

³ **Fledglings** are young birds that are ready to start flying.

As the summer months approach, the days grow warmer, and the warmer weather brings thermal updrafts.[1] Nox Gaak wants to play. Leaving her perch, she swoops down to her daughter feeding below. With the flick of a wing, Nox Gaak starts a chase, and soon after, the others follow. There's a spot nearby where the air lifts high above the trees when the weather is just right. Here, Nox Gaak can show off her acrobatic[2] flying, twisting and turning past all the others. These moments create a bond with her offspring as well as her mate.

WITH THE PACK

It is January, the time of K'uholxs, the Stories and Feasting Moon. This is the time of year when the Gitxsan celebrate the previous seasons of sustenance[1] and share stories that pass on teachings of life and thankfulness.

K'uholxs is the coldest part of the year, and Nox Gaak and the family of ravens have a hard time finding enough food. Ice and snow cover the land.

[1] **Sustenance** is the nourishment that sustains life, including food.

¹ To **succumb** is to give in to illness or to a stronger force; death.
² **Carrion** refers to the dead or decaying flesh of an animal.

A lone moose has succumbed¹ to the cold and lies frozen at the edge of a lake. Nox Gaak's daughter has found the carrion² and calls to her family. The ravens peck at the frozen moose with little success. The raven mother knows this won't be an easy feed, so she takes flight and travels across the valley to an area known only to her.

Nox Gaak rings out some calls that her offspring haven't heard before. After some time passes, she returns to the frozen moose and lands atop a leaning lodgepole pine. Soon, a small pack of wolves silently approaches the ravens. The raven mother knows this pack, and the wolves know her call.

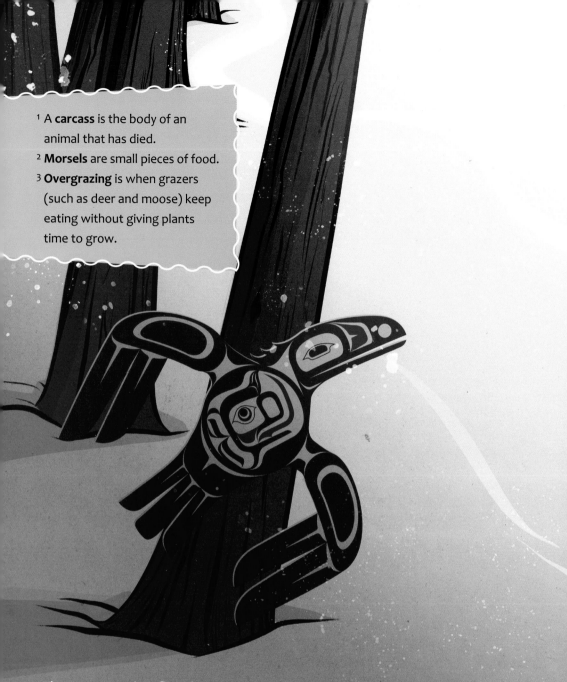

1. A **carcass** is the body of an animal that has died.
2. **Morsels** are small pieces of food.
3. **Overgrazing** is when grazers (such as deer and moose) keep eating without giving plants time to grow.

The raven mother flies down to the moose carcass[1] below, showing the wolves exactly where to go. The wolves are thankful for this meal. As their strong jaws crush the frozen moose, the ravens sneak through to grab the morsels[2] they couldn't get on their own.

The raven mother and the wolf mother are an unlikely pair. Yet through the ages, Nox Gaak and Nox Gibuu have helped each other, and in turn, they help the land. Each depends on the other to get through the winter. And as the raven's hoarding nature creates new life in the coming seasons, the wolves provide balance, keeping larger animals from overgrazing[3] the land. The Gitxsan view all life as being part of this sacred balance. One life cannot exist without all of the others.

The Gitxsan

The Gitxsan Nation are Indigenous peoples from unceded territories in the Northwest Interior of British Columbia. These 35,000 square kilometres of land cradle the headwaters of Xsan or "the River of Mists," also known by its colonial name, the Skeena River. The land defines who the Gitxsan people are.

The Nation follows a matrilineal line, and all rights, privileges, names, and stories come from the mothers. Lax Seel (Frog), Lax Gibuu (Wolf), Lax Skiik (Eagle), and Gisghaast (Fireweed) are the four clans of the people. It is taboo to marry a fellow clan member, even when there are no blood ties.

The four clans are divided among the territories by way of the Wilp system. A Wilp, or "house group," is a group comprising one or more families. Each Wilp has a Head Chief and Wing Chiefs, who are guided by Elders and members of their Wilp. Currently, there are 62 house groups, and each governs their portion of the Gitxsan Territories.

The Gitxsan Moons

K'uholxs	Stories and Feasting Moon	January
Lasa hu'mal	Cracking Cottonwood and Opening Trails Moon	February
Wihlaxs	Black Bear's Walking Moon	March
Lasa ya'a	Spring Salmon's Returning Home Moon	April
Lasa 'yan'tsa	Budding Trees and Blooming Flowers Moon	May
Lasa maa'y	Gathering and Preparing Berries Moon	June
Lasa 'wiihun	Fisherman's Moon	July
Lasa lik'i'nxsw	Grizzly Bear's Moon	August
Lasa gangwiikw	Groundhog Hunting Moon	September
Lasa xsin laaxw	Catching-Lots-of-Trout Moon	October
Lasa gwineekxw	Getting-Used-to-Cold Moon	November
Lasa 'wiigwineekxw or Lasa gunkw' ats	Severe Snowstorms and Sharp Cold Moon	December
Ax wa	Shaman's Moon	A blue moon, which is a second full moon in a single month

Kispiox
River

Stekyodin

Bulkley
River

Skeena River

Canada Council   Conseil des Arts
for the Arts   du Canada

We acknowledge the support of the Canada Council for the Arts.
Nous remercions le Conseil des arts du Canada de son soutien.

HighWater Press gratefully acknowledges the financial support of the Province of Manitoba through the Department of Sport, Culture and Heritage and the Manitoba Book Publishing Tax Credit, and the Government of Canada through the Canada Book Fund (CBF), for our publishing activities.

HighWater Press is an imprint of Portage & Main Press.
Printed and bound in Canada by Friesens
Design by Relish New Brand Experience
Cover Art by Natasha Donovan

Library and Archives Canada Cataloguing in Publication

Title: The raven mother / Hetxw'ms Gyetxw (Brett D. Huson) ; illustrated by Natasha Donovan.

Names: Huson, Brett D., author. | Donovan, Natasha, illustrator.
Series: Huson, Brett D. Mothers of Xsan ; 6.
Description: Series statement: Mothers of Xsan ; 6 | Includes some words in Gitxsanimx.
Identifiers: Canadiana (print) 20220259879 | Canadiana (ebook) 20220259887 | ISBN 9781774920039
  (hardcover) | ISBN 9781774920046 (EPUB) | ISBN 9781774920053 (PDF)
Subjects: LCSH: Ravens—Life cycles—Juvenile literature. | LCSH: Ravens—British Columbia—Juvenile
  literature. | LCSH: Indigenous peoples—British Columbia—Juvenile literature.
Classification: LCC QL696.P2367 H87 2022 | DDC j598.8/64—dc23

25 24 23 22   1 2 3 4 5

www.highwaterpress.com
Winnipeg, Manitoba
Treaty 1 Territory and homeland of the Métis Nation